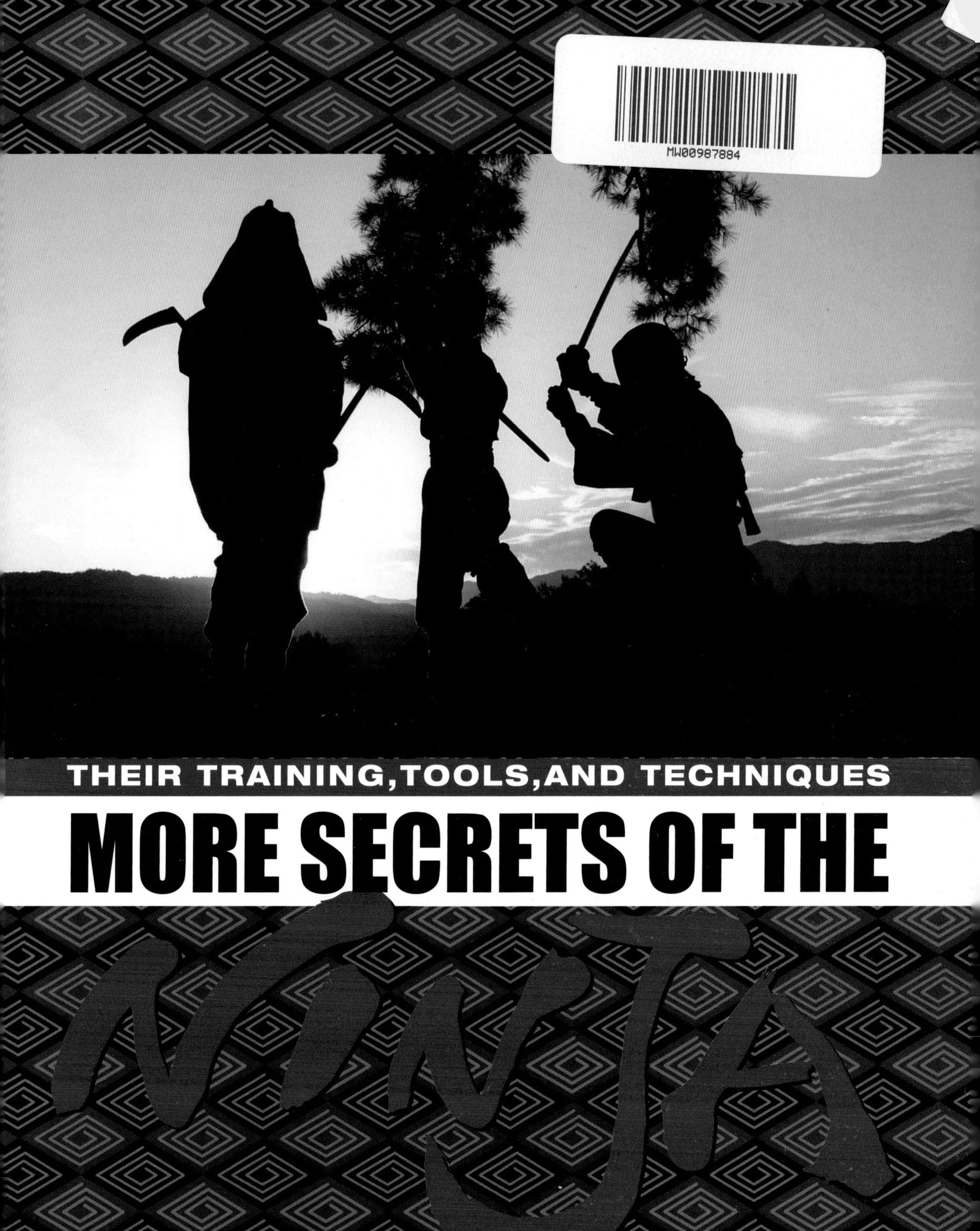

THEIR TRAINING, TOOLS, AND TECHNIQUES

MORE SECRETS OF THE NINJA

ABUNAI! DANGER!

Some of the skills, techniques, and weapons described in this book are dangerous and should NOT be tried at home or anywhere else. Please DO NOT harm yourself or anyone else by trying the moves it took decades for skilled professionals to master. By all means, meditate and enjoy as much *tofu* as your doctor feels is reasonable. But please DO NOT ambush your friends or start hurling *shuriken* around. If you want to learn more about *ninjutsu* or martial arts, we suggest you contact a school or *dojo* in your area. Neither DH Publishing nor any of its contributors accepts responsibility for damage or injury incurred attempting techniques described in this book.

MORE SECRETS OF THE NINJA

cocoro books

http://www.dhp-online.com

cocoro books is an imprint of DH Publishing, Inc.

CONTENTS

INTRODUCTION

The Secretive Ninja

By Brett Bull

For centuries, mystery has surrounded the existence of the ninja, the crafty, multi-talented sleuths of Japanese history. But if this were not the case, the interest in the weaponry, training, and lifestyle of these men of secrecy would likely be very little of what it is today.

The two kanji characters that make up the word "ninja" roughly translate to mean "stealth" and "person," which is appropriate given their traditional duties as assassins, spies, and scouts.

Modern curiosity in the ninja can be traced back to the end of World War II, a time when Japanese culture, as we envision it in its present state, was just beginning to move beyond its borders to the rest of the world.

Since then, ninja imagery and concepts have appeared in many forms of entertainment. Masashi Kishimoto created the popular manga series "Naruto," which chronicles the development of the main character, Naruto Uzumaki, as he trains and refines his ninja techniques while ascending to the role of leader of his village. Perhaps the wackiest adaptation of the ninja is the "Teenage Mutant Ninja Turtles" series of films that feature a fictional ninja team of four turtle mutants fighting evil-doers while living within the drainage system of Manhattan. In the James Bond film "You Only Live Twice," 007 battles a band of ninja assassins headed by the character Tiger Tanaka. And don't forget the Kawasaki "Ninja," the motorcycle whose ad copy often boasts--quite suitably given its name--of the machine's versatility.

While this modern view of the ninja might provide an overly agreeable impression, this amalgamation is quite dissimilar from the actual existence of its historical brethren.

Many historians will trace the earliest depictions of ninja-like activities to China in the 5th century BC, when Sun Tzu's warfare treatise "The Art of War" preached the use of secrecy and resourcefulness.

For Japan, certain texts have documented the existence of ninja teachings--such as the ability to outthink one's opponent--to as early as the 6th century, but it wasn't until nearly 1,000 years later that ninja were utilized extensively in combat.

In the 15th century, Japan was in a warring state in which feudal clans, overseen by a *daimyo* (lord), were constantly engaged in battle. The conventional warrior, the samurai, operated under the daimyo in accordance with the strict *bushido* code of conduct, which forbade concealment. Common lore says that this left the ninja, whose practice of *ninjutsu* (or the techniques of the ninja) resulted in expertise in stealth, dexterity and cunning, with numerous employment opportunities.

Two of the most recognizable clans of ninjutsu were the Koga-ryu and the Iga-ryu, both of which were named for mountainous regions in central Japan. Each daimyo often staffed his castle with a few dozen ninja, who worked on a freelance basis and usually hailed from tiny villages. Orders handed down by the daimyo included spreading misinformation, engaging in reconnaissance missions across enemy lines, and setting blazes within opposing fortifications. The hopeful outcome would be a garrison of enemy warriors fleeing their burning stronghold and plunging directly into the daimyo's waiting mob of armed samurai. Utilizing disguises, performing archery, and becoming adept at deploying explosives were also part of the ninja's arsenal.

The available weaponry was as varied as their duties. Swords and sharp throwing stars were the basics, while *shinobi-kumade* (iron hand claws) and *kagi-nawa* (hook rope) allowed for the scaling of walls and roofs. Simpler items, like small pouches and mesh bags, provided effective means for transporting tools and supplies.

Though the ninja is stereotyped to have dressed entirely in black, that wasn't always the case; clothing

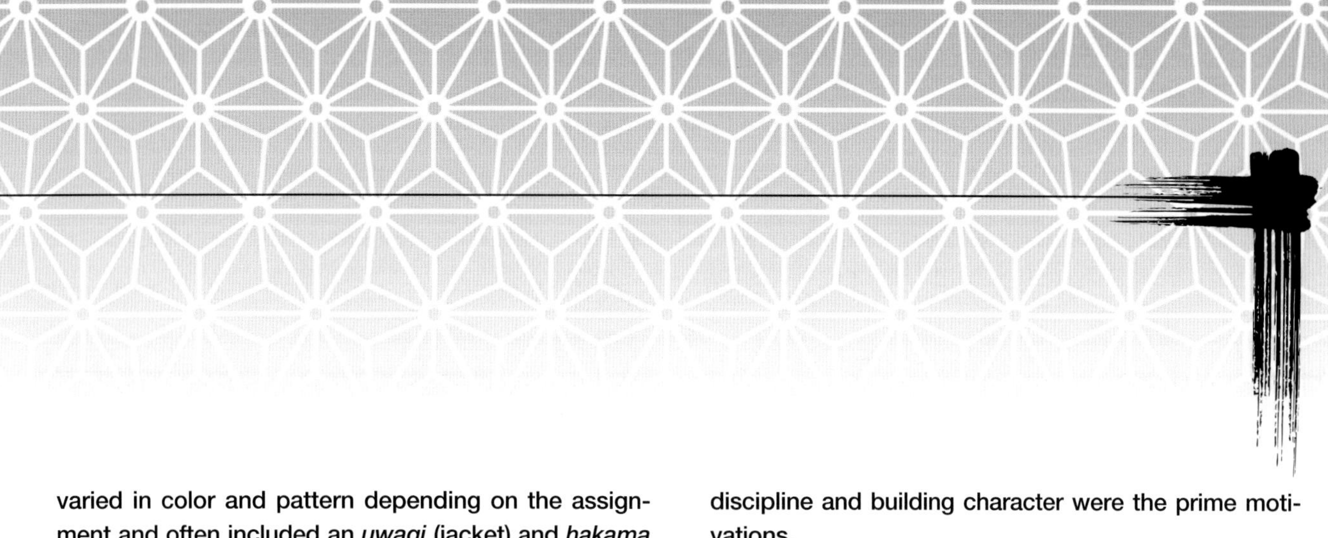

varied in color and pattern depending on the assignment and often included an *uwagi* (jacket) and *hakama* (pants), both of which must be fastened tightly to the body by gloves and leg wraps for sleek movement. A mask and hood covered the head, only allowing space for the eyes.

As the times changed, so did the techniques. With the beginning of the Edo Period (1603-1867), peace returned to Japan. As a consequence, the ninja were left without a significant source of revenue. Many turned to being bodyguards to the various daimyo, some even toting guns to coincide with advances in gunpowder.

The start of the Meiji Period (1868-1912) is generally considered the beginning of Japan's modern era. The government of the time focused its attention on the military, whose officers are said to have disliked the ninja for their secretive and shadowy ways. As a result, the ninja slowly migrated back to a humble existence in the villages of the countryside, where they performed rudimentary police work or utilized their skills in gunpowder to make fireworks.

Given this mercurial past, is it possible for a ninja to exist in modern times? While it would be highly dubious to assume that somewhere in Japan's mountainous regions reside a group of sly assassins, waiting on-call to creep up a castle's walls, there are indeed instructors and disciples of the art of ninjutsu.

The thin yet spry grandmaster Masaaki Hatsumi is considered by many to be the last ninja. Hatsumi trained under Toshitsugu Takamatsu, the legendary last "fighting ninja" who is said to have won 12 fights to the death and gouged out the eyeballs of one of his attackers.

Following World War II, many traditional martial arts were prohibited by the Allied Occupation. When the ban was lifted in 1948, a boom in the study of empty-handed forms like judo and karate resulted. Instilling discipline and building character were the prime motivations.

Hatsumi, born on December 2, 1931 began studying martial arts and Japanese weaponry in his youth. His first lessons with Takamatsu, who didn't believe in warm-ups during training since fights unfolded at a moment's notice, took place in 1957. For 15 years, Hatsumi traveled 15 hours each week to train with Takamatsu, who Hatsumi has described in interviews as the man who taught him that the most important thing in survival is understanding defeat.

Today, Hatsumi teaches in his Bujinkan *dojo* in Japan's Chiba Prefecture. Hatsumi, who preaches self-discipline, balance, and the continual exploitation of an opponent's vulnerabilities, such as arrogance, takes his students through various moves and motions with swords and other standard ninja gear. On his *tatami* mats, the grandmaster has taught numerous U.S. soldiers, police officers and members of the FBI and CIA. For the filming of "You Only Live Twice," he worked as a martial arts consultant.

Though a recent decline in interest in the martial arts in Japan has relegated ninjutsu to not much more than a curiosity--baseball and soccer are commonly played by school children--many ninjutsu schools throughout the United States and Europe owe their existence to the teachings of Hatsumi.

In many of his books, such as "Essence of Ninjutsu" and "The Way of the Ninja: Secret Techniques," Hatsumi attempts to explain the essence and truth of ninja principles by emphasizing mental strength and intellectual understanding. While modern Japan--and the rest of the world for that matter--likely has little use for the daredevil ninja of old, such concepts could be applicable to nearly any time, place or activity--and perhaps that then is the real charm of the ninja.

Throwing a chain and sickle on the end of an enemy's sword makes it yours.

In combat the sickle could prove as deadly as the sword.

Castle walls did little to stop the spider-like ninja.

The ninja's constant training made them extremely fast on his feet.

With two sickles, the ninja pinions his enemy.

Pressed against a wall, the ninja listens in on his enemies.

The *kusari-gama* was a chain with two sickles on the end. Like a flying blender, it was deadly effective against the enemy.

A pair of metal hoops with sharp teeth on the inner and outer edge were used for fighting.

Even a length of rope became a deadly weapon in the hands of the ninja.

Clothes, Equipment, Codes, Exercise, and Stealth

THE BASICS

A few things a ninja needs before heading over the palace walls.

BACK IN BLUE: THE UNIFORM

Wash and wear versatility-- it moves, it camouflages, and it never goes out of style.

When we think of the ninja stalking their victim at night, we imagine them dressed all in black. In fact, dark blue was the first color of choice. In the bright moonlight, black stands out like a sore thumb. Other colors in the ninja wardrobe included brown and gray, which they would don according to the brightness of the moon. They also kept a set of reversible clothes, which allowed for an immediate disguise if spotted by the enemy.

The Outfit

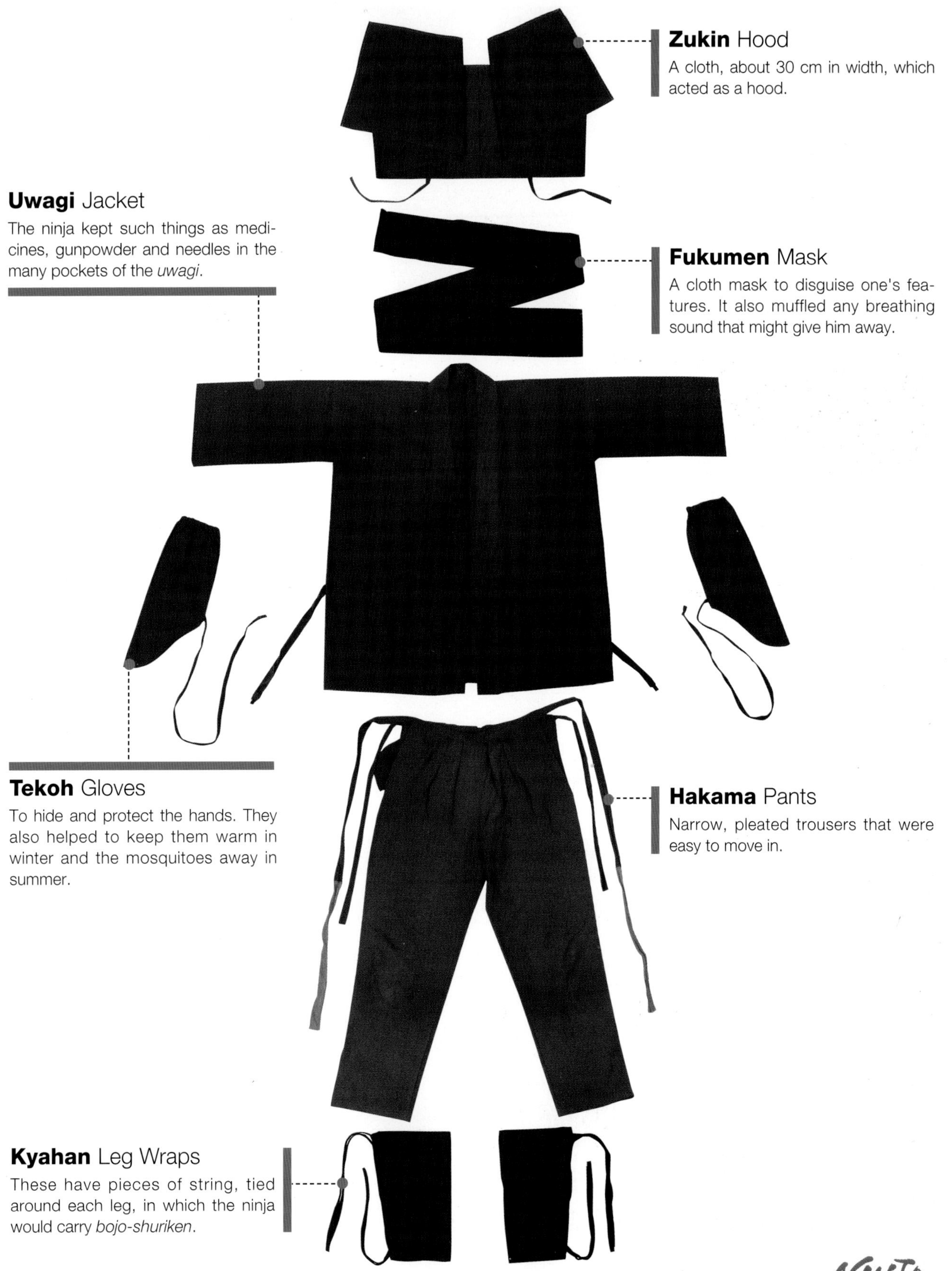

Zukin Hood

A cloth, about 30 cm in width, which acted as a hood.

Uwagi Jacket

The ninja kept such things as medicines, gunpowder and needles in the many pockets of the *uwagi*.

Fukumen Mask

A cloth mask to disguise one's features. It also muffled any breathing sound that might give him away.

Tekoh Gloves

To hide and protect the hands. They also helped to keep them warm in winter and the mosquitoes away in summer.

Hakama Pants

Narrow, pleated trousers that were easy to move in.

Kyahan Leg Wraps

These have pieces of string, tied around each leg, in which the ninja would carry *bojo-shuriken*.

Getting Dressed

1 Put on the *uwagi*.

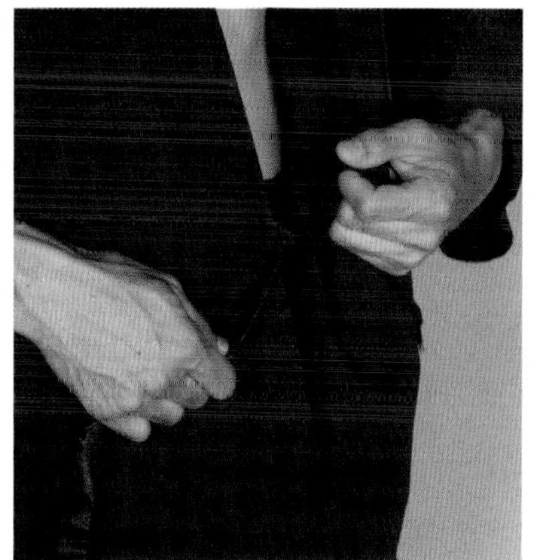

2 Tie the inside strings to tighten the waist.

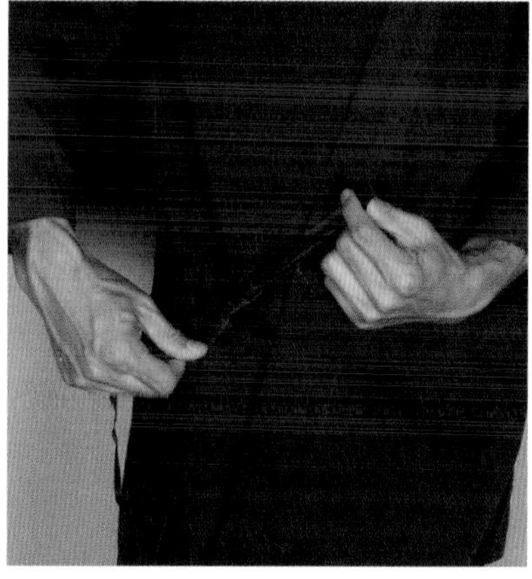

3 Hold the left side over the right, and tie the strings in front.

4 Put on the *hakama*. Pull the string from behind across the chest and tie. Tuck in the *uwagi*.

5 Pull up the front part of the *hakama*. Wrap the string once around the body and tie at the front.

6 Insert a nail into each knot so it doesn't come undone.

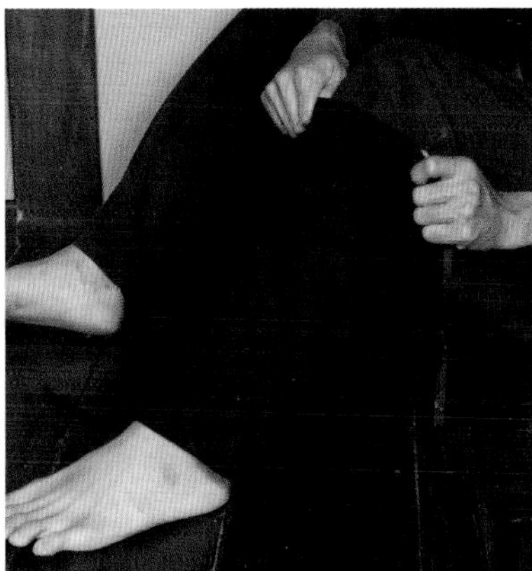

7 Tie the *kyahan* to the left leg. Like the *samurai*, the ninja must be prepared at all times for a sudden attack.

8 The upper strings of the *kyahan* are tied just below the knee. A nail is tied onto the loose ends.

9 The lower strings of the *kyahan* are tied around the ankle. Again, a nail is tied onto the loose ends.

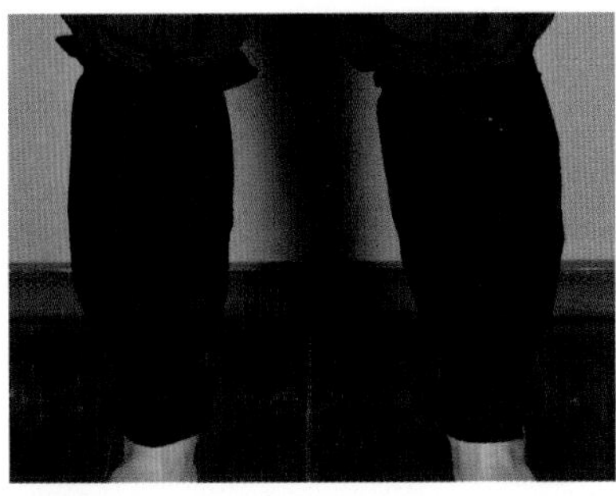

10 In the same manner, tie the *kya-han* to the right leg. The legs are now done.

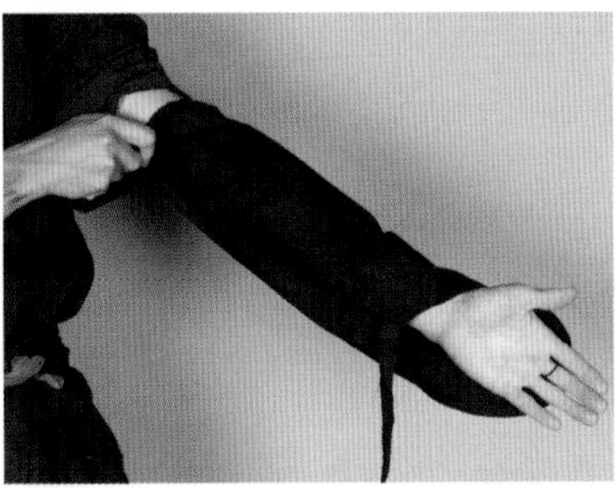

11 Put the *tekoh* on, starting with the left hand.

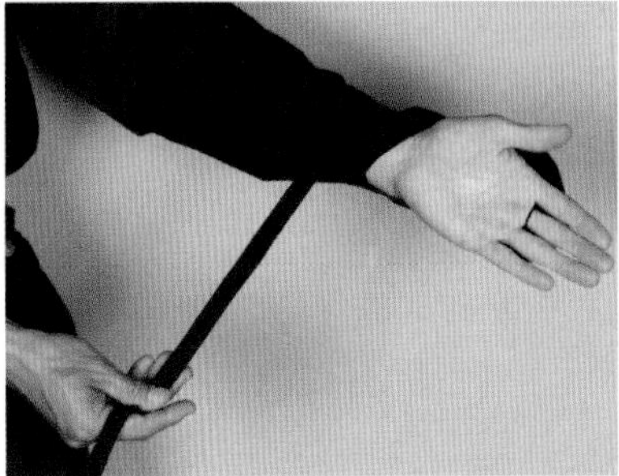

12 The *tekoh*'s string has a bead on the end. After wrapping the string around the wrist a number of times, insert this bead underneath. Do the same with the right hand.

13 Put on the *fukumen* making sure to completely cover the nose, mouth, and chin.

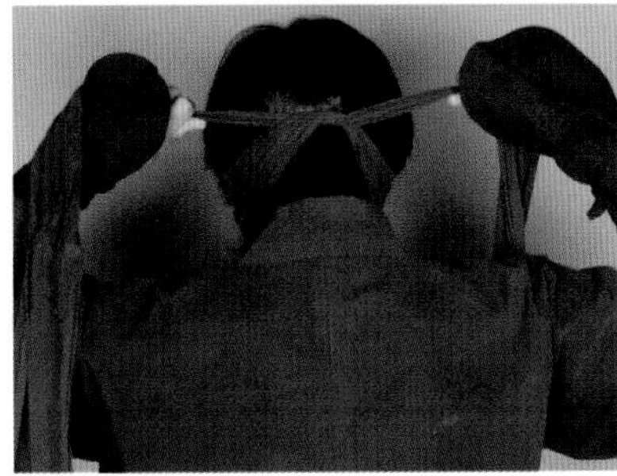

14 Make sure the *fukumen* is firmly tied at the back.

15 Place the *zukin* so that the front part hangs down over the eye-brows. Tie the string at the back.

16 Cover the head with the rest of the *zukin*.

17 To conceal the ears, pull the sides down and cross them under the chin.

18 Tie them firmly behind the head. Voila, dressed to kill.

FINISH

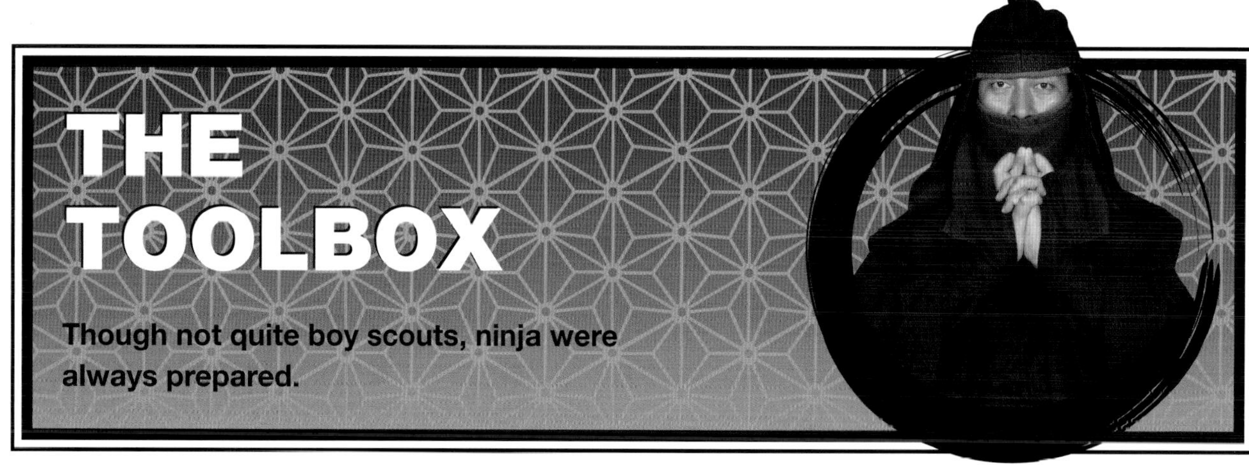

THE TOOLBOX

Though not quite boy scouts, ninja were always prepared.

Weapons and Tools

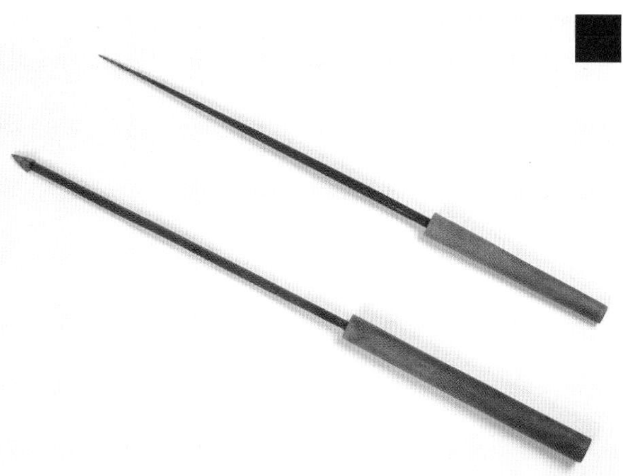

Tsui-giri Picks
Large picks used for both fighting and carving spyholes in walls.

Torinoko Smoke Bomb
Gunpowder was wrapped with a sheet of paper like a firecracker, and a paper fuse was attached. It could be used as a hand grenade or smokescreen.

Maru-kagi Round Key
Another item for jimmying open a big lock.

Ibushi-ki Smoke Pot
A flute-like ceramic cylinder with eight holes along the side and one at the top. When gunpowder was poured in and lit, a curtain of smoke rose from the holes.

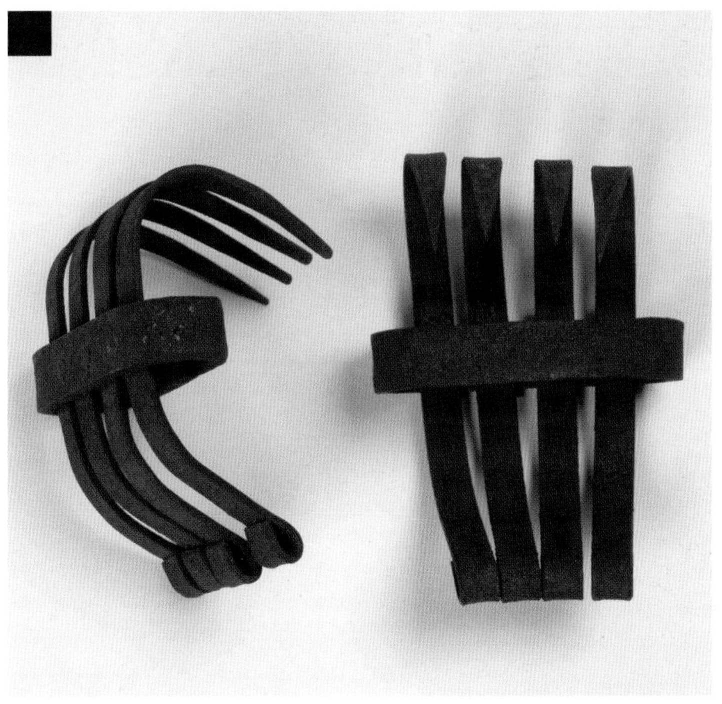

Tekko-kagi Iron Claws

A multi-purpose instrument: In battle it could be used as defense against a sword, and when scaling walls it could be attached to the hand like a four-spike crampon.

Kagi-nawa Hook Rope

Just like the grappling hook, this was used for climbing up and getting down.

Ikari-kagi Grappling Hook

Tied to the end of a rope, this metal anchor would be thrown over walls or onto roofs, allowing the ninja to go up and away.

Uchi-kagi Prying Hook

Held in both hands, the hook was driven into a wall to help the ninja climb. It could also be used to open doors.

Kiri Pick

Smaller than the one on the market, this easy-to-conceal blade was used to cut holes.

Maki-hashigo Roll-up Ladder

The pointed, top part of this portable pulley was thrown over a wall, and the rest drawn up like a bucket from a well.

Odds and Ends

Missho-ire
Secret Document Holder
Made to look like the sheath of a small sword, it contains instead a pipe in which secret documents could be concealed from the enemy.

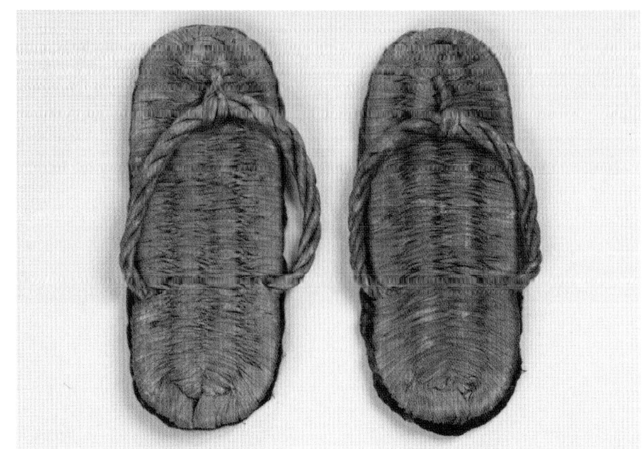

Zouri Sandals
A style of slipper made of plaited rope with cotton soles. Used for walking in absolute silence.

Hoguchi Tinder Box
This box kept hot coals. Just a pinch was needed to start a fire.

Seoi-bukuro Shoulder Bag
The ninja's daypack was a net bag of strong rope for carrying tools. He slung it over his left shoulder to allow the right hand freedom of movement.

Tenohira-taimatsu
Hand-held Torch
This compact torch was made from pine resin and bamboo skin, keeping it alight even in the rain.

Gando Search Light
A kind of flashlight in which a candle is cleverly fixed to two hoopes that move, keeping the candle upright at any angle.

Tobacco-ire Tobacco Pouch

The ninja used this pouch not for tobacco but for gunpowder. On the job the ninja was a non-smoker -- the smell would have given him away.

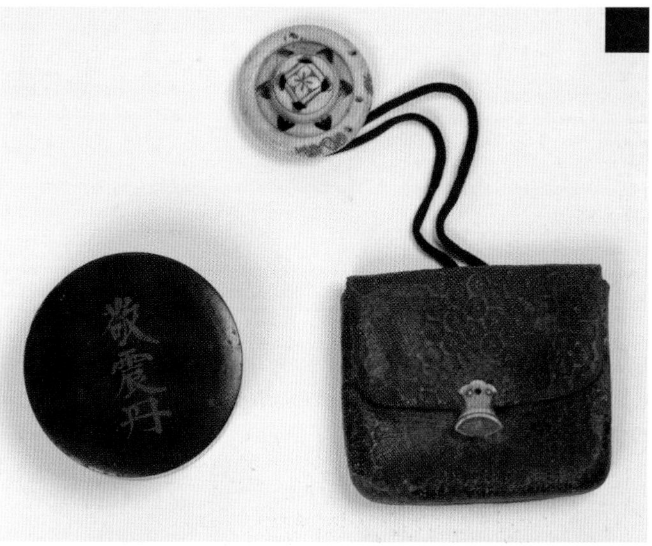

Kusuri-ire Medicine Pouch

These kinds of pouches were used by ordinary people as well. The left one bears the name of the medicine. The right one has the *kamon*, or family crest on it.

TALKING THE TALK:CODES AND SIGNS

Here's how to get the message without blowing your cover.

Passwords

In the cloak and dagger world that the ninja inhabited, telling friend from foe could mean the difference between life and death. This is where passwords came into play, instrumental at such times as delivering secret documents or contacting allies behind enemy lines. The words they used -- motifs from nature, poetic associations, antonyms -- they borrowed from the vernacular, modifying them on a daily basis to avoid detection.

Such passwords included word associations in nature:

Japanese	Japanese in English	English
山—森	Yama—Mori	**Mountain—Forest**
日—月	Hi—Tsuki	**Sun—Moon**
花—実	Hana—Mi	**Flower—Fruit**
海—塩	Umi—Shio	**Sea—Salt**
谷—水	Tani—Mizu	**Valley—Water**
火—煙	Hi—Kemuri	**Fire—Smoke**
山—川	Yama—Kawa	**Mountain—River**

Passwords were also taken from poems such as tanka:

Japanese	Japanese in English	English
雪—富士	Yuki—Fuji	**Snow—Mt. Fuji**
花—吉野	Hana—Yoshino	**Flower—Yoshino** (a region for flowers)
煙—浅間	Kemuri—Asama	**Smoke—Mt. Asama** (a volcano)
萩—宮城野	Hagi—Miyashirono	**Bush Clover—Miyashirono** (another flower region)

Secret Code

Secret messages were conveyed with the use of elaborate codes that would be overlooked by anyone but the recipient. The ninja's ploys included rice grains dyed different colors (*goshikimai*), knotted rope (*yuinawa-moji*), and letters that only their allies could understand.

Goshiki-mai Five-Color Rice

Rice grains were dyed blue, yellow, red, black or purple and arranged in different combinations or patterns. With this technique, the ninja could make over 100 different codes.

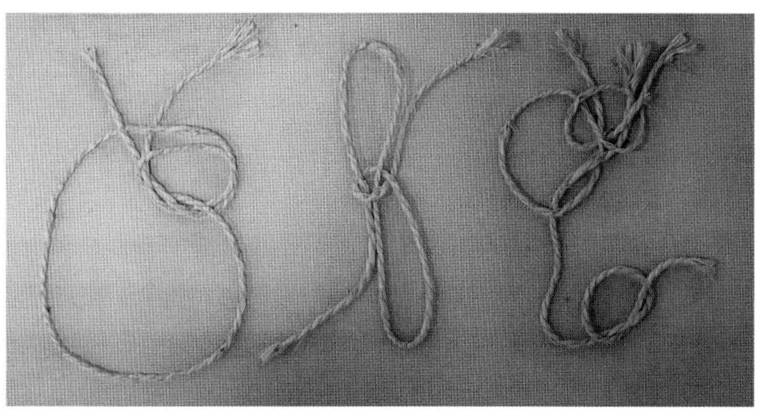

Yuinawa-moji Rope-Code

Rope with a particular number or style of knots could serve as a coded message. These would be hung in conspicuous places, such as from the eaves of a roof.

栬 i	⿰火色 ro	⿰土色 ha	銫 ni	⿰氵色 ho	⿰亻色 he	⿰身色 to
棈 chi	⿰火青 ri	埥 nu	錆 ru	清 wo	倩 wa	⿰身青 ka
横 yo	熿 ta	⿰土黄 re	鐄 so	潢 tsu	僙 ne	⿰身黄 na
⿰木赤 ra	⿰火赤 mu	⿰土赤 u	⿰金赤 i	浾 no	⿰亻赤 o	⿰身赤 ku
柏 ya	⿰火白 ma	⿰土白 ke	鉑 fu	泊 ko	伯 e	⿰身白 te
⿰木黒 a	⿰火黒 se	⿰土黒 ki	⿰金黒 yu	潶 me	⿰亻黒 mi	⿰身黒 shi
⿰木紫 e	⿰火紫 hi	⿰土紫 mo	⿰金紫 se	⿰氵紫 su	⿰亻紫 n	⿰身紫 —

Shinobi-iroha Ninja Alphabet

The ninja made their own 48 letters with a combination of parts of Chinese characters. These 48 letters were used as secret codes for *Iga* and *Koga* ninjas.

ワ wa	ラ ra	ヤ ya	マ ma	ハ ha
ヰ i	リ ri	ヰ i	ミ mi	ヒ hi
ウ u	ル ru	ユ yu	ム mu	フ hu
ヱ e	レ re	ヱ e	メ me	ヘ he
ヲ wo	ロ ro	ヨ yo	モ mo	ホ ho

ナ na	タ ta	サ sa	カ ka	ア a
ニ ni	チ chi	シ si	キ ki	イ i
ヌ nu	ツ tsu	ス su	ク ku	ウ u
ネ ne	テ te	セ se	ケ ke	エ e
ノ no	ト to	ソ so	コ ko	オ o

These were letters used in ancient Japan before the ideogramatic system (*kanji*) was introduced. They made an ideal code as few, if anyone, could understand them.

THE NINJA WORKOUT

Ever see a flabby ninja? Didn't think so. This regimen kept them in fighting condition.

Full Body Workout

1. Get into the push-up position with the fists clenched.
2. From the push-up position, push up off of the ground with the toes. It's harder than it looks.

Aural Workout

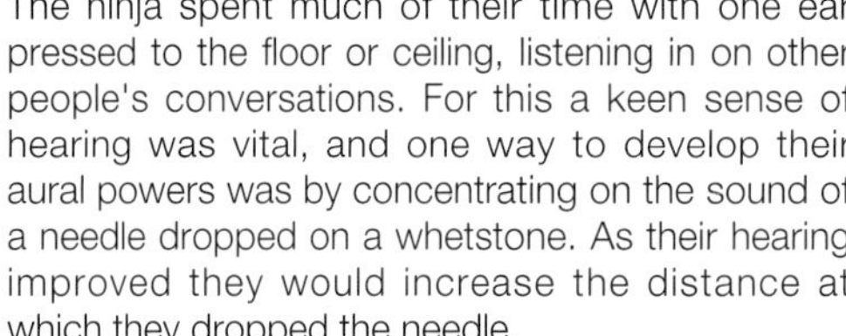

The ninja spent much of their time with one ear pressed to the floor or ceiling, listening in on other people's conversations. For this a keen sense of hearing was vital, and one way to develop their aural powers was by concentrating on the sound of a needle dropped on a whetstone. As their hearing improved they would increase the distance at which they dropped the needle.

Visual Workout

To improve eyesight, the ninja had a number of peculiar techniques. One was to stare for long periods of time at the flame of a candle. Ouch. Another was to walk back and forth between a dark room and a lit one to enable his eyes to adjust quickly in sudden changes of light.

Strengthening the Arms

The ninja's hands and arms were weapons and they needed to be kept in perfect condition. They would work the arms, shoulders and fingers by hanging from a branch until they dropped.

Strengthening the Fingers

1. Open the hand and extend the arm.
2. Bend the first and second joint of each finger.
3. In that position, clench the fingers tight. Do this repeatedly to strengthen the fingers and the hand's grip.

Jump Training

1. Dig a hole and stand in it. Really.
2. Without bending the knees, jump out. Begin with a shallow hole of about 3 cm deep, and gradually make it deeper. With constant training the ninja was able to leap nimbly over an assailant.

WALK LIKE A NINJA

Move with maximum speed and stealth on any turf.

Shinobi-ashi
On Tiptoe

This is perhaps the easiest of the ninja walks. Without making a sound, begin by placing your fourth toe on the ground and immediately follow up with the middle toe, and then lastly your heel.

Uki-ashi
Floating Foot

For this one, you walk only on the tips of your toes, with your heels never touching the floor. Although perfect for a sneak attack, it can be pretty tough on the toes.

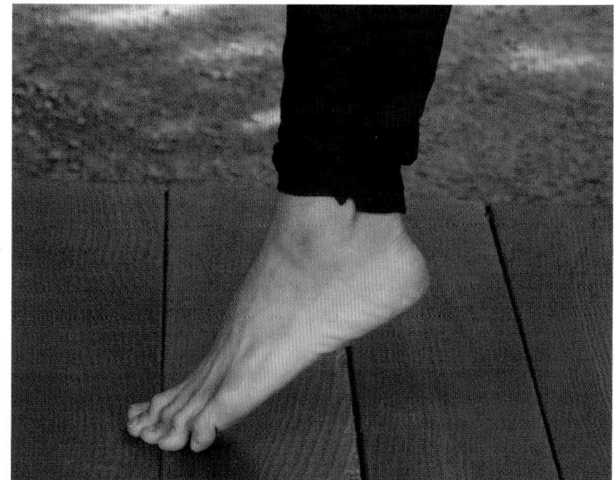

Inu-bashiri
Dog Walk

This method is used to creep through low places on all-fours, like a dog. Drop down to your hands and knees, then alternately place your hands firmly on the ground and move forward.

Kitsune-bashiri
Fox Walk

Like the Dog Walk, this is also on all-fours. However, it's a fox-like noiseless scamper on only the toes and fingertips. You'll really need to train your toes and fingers to master this walk.

Yoko-bashiri
Sideways Walk

First press your back firmly against the wall. Then, facing the direction you want to go in, open your arms and legs out as wide as you can. Cross your far leg and arm over your forward ones and repeat, sidling along like a crab. This allows you to travel further with fewer steps.

Shin-so-toh-ho
Deep Grass Rabbit Walk

In the most silent of methods, you place the balls of your feet on the backs of your hands and, bent over in that position, walk forward on your hands. It requires many years' practice and a lot of stamina.

Meditation and Ninjutsu

THE MOVES

Old-school ninja martial arts for dispatching enemies and living to tell about it.

MEDITATION

Fire up your *Ki* for battle or unwind after a long day of toppling shogun.

In is most effective for calming and relaxing the mind.

In would be performed each morning and evening.

The ninja's life was one of physical danger and mental stress. You can imagine. To overcome these hardships, they practiced a form of meditation using symbols known as *In*. They combined this with a method of autosuggestion called *Kuji Goshin-hou*, which they believed gave them certain powers. The roots of *In* lay in receiving spiritual energy from the sun and the moon. As the sun rose at dawn they would face the sun; in the evening, they would look toward the moon. Even before battle, the ninja practiced this meditation.

The Kuji Goshin-hou In Technique

Rin

Press the palms of both hands together and lock the fingers. Raise the index fingers so they stand together.

Pyou

Raise the middle finger. Coil the index finger around it.

Tou

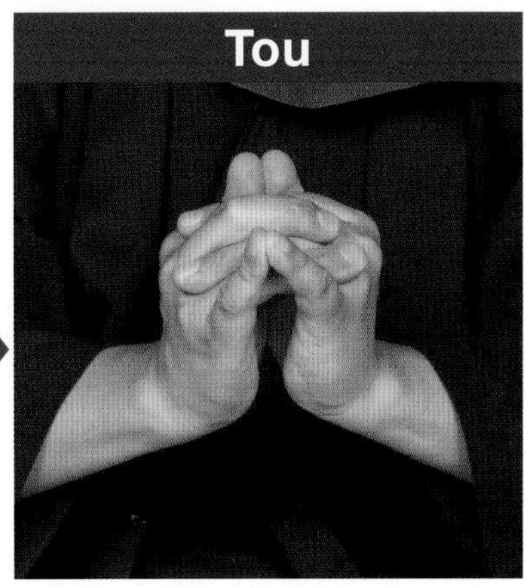

As with the *Rin* technique, lock the fingers of both hands together. Raise the thumbs so they stand touching. Now do the same with the little fingers.

Sha

Press the palms of both hands together and lock the fingers below the palms. Raise the index fingers so they stand together.

Kai

Place the flat of the palms and fingers together as in prayer.

Jin

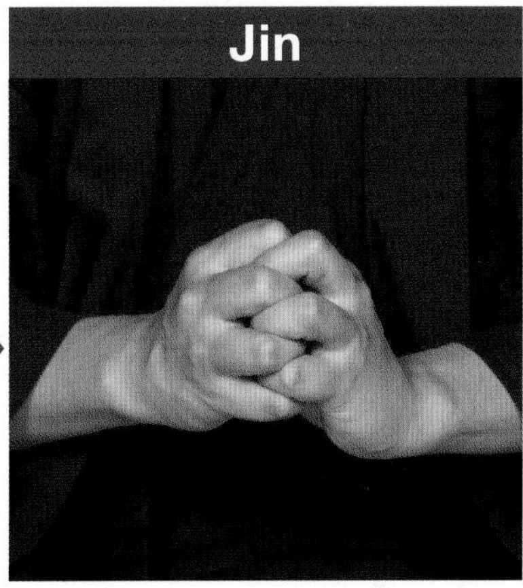

Lock the fingers together below the palms, so that the knuckles join.

Retsu

With the thumb sticking up, clench the fingers of the right hand. With the left hand, grasp the thumb of the right.

Zai

Press the tips of the thumbs together while holding the hands apart with the fingers spread open.

Zen

Lightly clench the left hand. Rest it in the right hand.

Toh-in

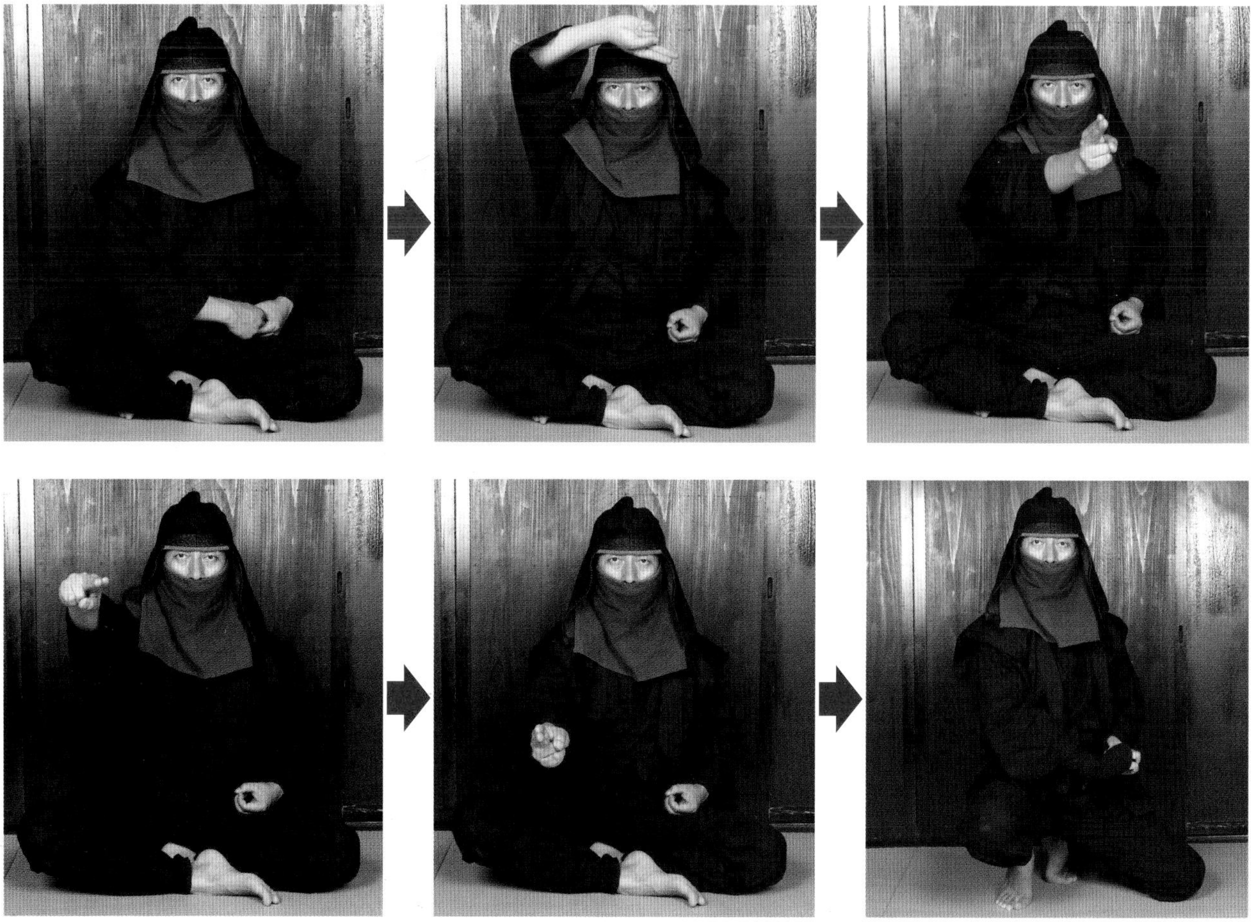

This technique was developed from the hand exercises of *Kuji Goshin-hou* to increase the ninja's power. It was practiced with a sword or, when no sword was available, with the left hand. He would begin by shouting "Ah!" while swinging his sword down in a vertical motion. This would be followed by "Ki!" as his sword cut through the air in a horizontal swing. With this introduction over, he would continue swinging his sword vertically then horizontally as he recited the rest of the mantra -- "Sa! Ta! Ka! Ha! Wa! Ya! E!"

Norito

When praying for the health of his family and safety on his travels, or more immediate concerns, such as favorable weather or recovery from injury, the ninja would swing his sword just like for *Toh-in* while chanting, "So Ra Chi Yu Ra Chi Ku Ku Re Ah."

Juji-hou

For more power, the ninja would combine *Kuji Goshin-hou* with *Juji-hou*. He would practice *Kuji Goshin-hou* and then draw a wish in one word.

NINJUTSU: FIGHTING, HIDING, AND MAKING A GETAWAY

Centuries of fighting dirty have yielded great techniques for both offense and defense.

Martial Arts

Kagi-nawa Hook Rope

1 Hold a bundle of rope in the left hand to block the enemy's attack or just use it to trip him up.

2 Using your other hand, strike the enemy in the belly and drive the hook into his clothes and flesh.

3 With his sword now out of action, you make your move, strangling him with one left twist of the rope while pinning his right arm firmly against your body.

4 While twisting your opponent's arm, move behind him and tie his arm behind him. He'll be unable to move without the hook digging deeper into his wound.

Kanawa Fighting Hoops

1 The *kanawa* is a set of hoops with nasty notched blades attached to the inside and out (the handle area is wrapped in cloth). As your opponent wields his sword, swing the *kanawa* into action.

2 Catch the attacker's sword in the teeth of the *kanawa*, and you can pull him off his feet.

3 To trap him, bring the *kanawa* down over his arms.

4 Step back and hook the other *kanawa* around his neck, immobilizing him, or finish him off.

Mantoh Shears

1 Traditionally used for cutting branches, this large pair of shears is only referred to as *mantoh* when used as a weapon. The handles are gripped tightly as you lunge at your enemy.

2 The blades are then opened, and held horizontally to scissor your attacker's sword as it swings in for the kill.

3 You then give it a twist to knock him off balance.

4 Step in to trap and hold him with the blades around his neck, or just snip him like a daisy.

Tekagi Metal Claw

1 Although the *tekagi*, a set of four metal claws worn on the hand, was originally used by farmers for gathering grass, it doubles as a nasty ninja weapon.

2 When meeting your enemy, conceal your *tekagi* hand in your clothes.

3 With your free hand try to block the swing of his sword.

4 Immediately, attack his sword arm with the *tekagi*, rendering it badly mauled and unable to hold a sword.

5 Take him out in one swipe by going for a weak point like the neck or face.

Nicho-gama Sickle

1 The *nicho-gama*, a type of sickle, is yet another farmer's implement used with deadly effect by ninja. Makes you wonder about farmers. One is usually held in each hand. When attacked, the left-hand sickle catches the swinging sword.

2 You then bring the right-hand sickle down hard between your opponent's hands on the sword.

3 Follow this with an upward twist to quickly relieve him of his sword.

4 Quickly move behind him so the two sickles can be slashed across his neck for the coup de grace.

Chigirigi Staff

1 The *chigirigi* is a weapon cunningly disguised as a blind man's staff.

2 First, use the *chigirigi* to deflect the attacker's sword.

3 When he tries to strike again, whip the sword down and out of harm's way with the chain hidden inside the stick.

4 Flip him over with your foot, and push him to the ground with the stick.

5 Take his short sword away and stab him with it.

Shakujou Walking Stick

1 The *shakujou* is another seemingly harmless implement used as a walking stick by itinerant Buddhists in the mountains.

2 The stick can stop a sword mid-swing.

3 Hook the metal point at the top of the stick onto your opponent's hilt or fingers. Pull back to take his sword away.

4 You then stab your opponent with the stick, back away, and grab his sword.

5 Once you've knocked aside the smaller blade he has drawn, you move in for the kill with your new sword.

Kusari-gama(Male)

Ball and Chain

1 *Kusari* is a type of chain. Add a weight at one end and a sickle at the other, and you've got a *kusari-gama*. Swung with force, it will make any assailant back off.

2 Gentlemen, to knock him off his feet, simply whack him across the head with the weight.

3 Now that he's off-balance, wrap the chain around his sword.

4 Pull the chain up and over his head, so that his sword is against his back.

5 Once he's tied up with the chain, you can take his short sword and deliver the fatal wound.

Kusari-gama(Female)

Ball and Chain

1 Ladies, first deflect the strike of your attacker's sword with the *kusari-gama* held in the right hand.

2 As the sword is knocked down, swing at his neck with the chain.

3 With the chain now coiled around his neck, pull it tight to choke him.

4 Step behind him to avoid his flailing sword and finish him off with the sickle. You go, girl.

Jumonji-nawa

Figure Ten or Cross Rope

1 This technique allows you to snare your opponent with a length of rope and a bamboo pipe. Beforehand, fill the bamboo pipe with an eye irritant. When your assailant appears, blow the powder into his eyes.

2 While he's temporarily blinded, pummel him with your fists to knock the sword out of his hand, then throw the noose around his neck.

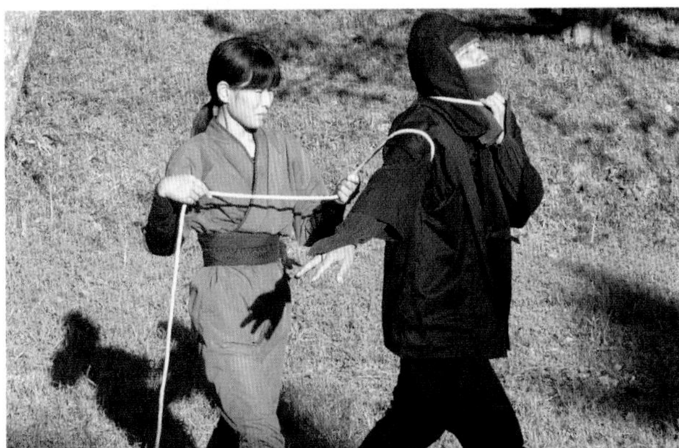

3 Tugging on the rope to strangle him, loop the other end around his right arm.

4 At the same time, put his left hand through the loop to form a figure "∞" on his back.

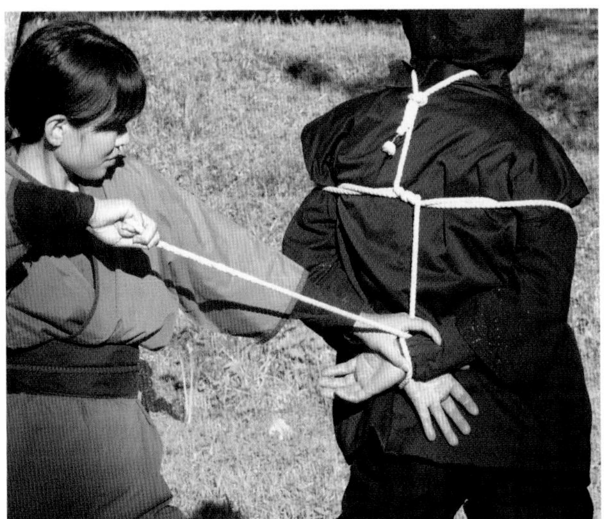

5 Wind the rope at the center of his back, and tie his wrists behind him. The rope forms a cross, the *kanji* for ten.

Tobi-nawa

Flying Rope

1 Before the fight, throw a length of rope over a branch of a tree, and hide the coil behind you.

2 Block his sword with your arm.

3 Smash his hand with your knee to make him drop his sword.

4 Smash your elbow into his back to bring him down hard, then deftly loop the rope around his neck.

5 Pull the other end of the rope to hoist him off his feet. Tie it to the tree, and hang him high.

Ebi-nawa Shrimp Rope

1 To start off, jump out of the way of your opponents striking sword and bring your elbow down onto the hilt.

2 Now grab his arm with your right hand, and knee him hard in the solar plexus.

3 Grab the opponent's wrist from behind and pull his arm hard. This should make him drop his sword.

4 Throw the noose that you've already prepared over his right hand and pull it tight.

5 Loop the other end around his left leg and again pull tight until he's bent backwards like a cooked shrimp.

Gyaku-hachimonji-nawa

Upside-down Figure Eight Rope

1 Begin by rendering your assailant sword-less with a smash of your knee to the back of his hand.

2 Kick him hard in the stomach to double him up in pain, and then slip the noose of the rope over his right hand.

3 Yank the arm up and down behind his back.

4 From behind, loop the rope around his neck.

5 Twist his left arm behind his back and truss it up tight. The rope should now form a V-shape (or the inverted *kanji* character for "eight").

Ichimonji-nawa Figure One Rope

1 From the side, bring your knee up hard on your opponent's arm. This surprise should cause him to drop his sword.

2 A swift kick to the stomach will knock him off his feet, allowing you to slip the noose around his right wrist. These moves are the same as *gyaku-hachimonji-nawa*.

3 Yank his right elbow up over his sholder.

4 From behind, put noose over his left wrist and pull tight. The result should resemble a number "1."

Mutoh-dori Bare-handed

1 When sure of where your attacker's sword is heading, lunge forward and grab the hilt with both hands.

2 Drag his arms and sword down to the ground hard.

3 Without letting go, clasp your legs around his arms and twist them down.

4 In this position, hold his arms with your legs, snatch the sword, and stab him to death.

Fukiya Blow Pipe

1 This ingenious weapon is a type of blow-pipe that uses a dart made from a sewing needle wrapped in paper. It is extremely accurate. The tip of the needle is dipped in a poison, such as aconite, which kills the victim before he can even open his mouth.

2 Put a rolled sheet of paper inside a flute which you can use in a disguise, and place the needle inside the paper.

3 Seal the note holes with your fingers, and assess the enemy's position.

4 Stand with your legs apart for balance. Place the flute to your mouth. Aim with your left hand at the end of the flute. And then, with one strong puff, shoot the dart at the unsuspecting victim.

Shuriken

In combat, a distance of three or four meters puts the swordsman at a clear disadvantage. This is the time to break out the *shuriken*. From cross-shaped weapons to spikes, these flying weapons come in different shapes and sizes, and can be thrown from a standing, sitting or lying position.

Shiho-shuriken Four Point Shuriken

1 The *shiho-shuriken* has four sharp points. When throwing, one point is clasped in the hand while the extended forefinger rests over another. Only the top of the point is sharpened to prevent injury from throwing it.

2 It is thrown from the right hand held high. The left hand is held out in front to guage the distance of the target.

3 As the left hand is pulled back, the weapon is thrown overhand from the right. Put a forward spin on it with the extended finger as it leaves the hand.

Bojo-shuriken Spike Shuriken

1 This *shuriken* is shaped like a spike. There are two ways to throw this *shuriken*. One is called *jika-uchi*, where you throw it sharp end forward. The other is *han-uchi*, where you throw it the other way around.

2 Basically the arm action is same as *shiho-shuriken*. For short distances, throw it *jika-uchi*. For long distances, throw it *han-uchi*.

3 As the throwing arm swings down into a horizontal position, the thumb's grip loosens, releasing the weapon.

Yonoyami-uchi Double-Shuriken Throw

This is the technique for throwing two *shuriken* at the same time but for two different distances. It is used at night or when the enemy's distance is hard to determine.

Nawa & Kama Sickle Grappling Hook

1 The combination of these simple tools can be very effective when scaling high walls. Affix three sickles angled 120 degrees apart to form a grappling hook, and tie them to the end of a long piece of rope.

2 Face the wall and throw the grappling hook over so it snags a roof-tile.

3 With foot-loops knotted into the rope, you can easily shimmy up and over the wall.

Rikuzen Iron Bar

1 Force the iron bar into stone walls where fingers and toes won't fit to climb up.

2 Make sure it's secure, and put your weight on it to climb up.

3 Repeating the method, make your way to the top step by step.

Free Climbing

1 The only tools here are your feet, hands, and the strength in your fingers. This method is most effective when climbing cliffs or old stone walls.

2 Pull yourself up by gripping protrusions or finger-holes in the wall.

3 Make sure that what you're holding isn't loose, then crawl up like a spider.

Tenton-juppou

The technique of using weather conditions and natural phenomena -- bright sunlight, snow, wind, mist, etc.-- to escape danger.

Nitton Mirror

An ingenious distraction to allow you a surprise escape. When the enemy is between you and the sun, use a small hand mirror to reflect the light into his eyes. When his vision returns, you're gone.

Chiton-juppou

The technique of using natural elements, such as fire, soil, metal or wood, to escape your enemies.

Souton
Tripwire

By tying long strands of grass together, you can make natural tripwires.

Doton
Blinding

Throwing sand or gravel in your enemy's face and eyes will temporarily blind him while you make a run for it.

Enton
Cloud of smoke

Smoke bombs were made from a mix of saltpeter, sulphur, charcoal and camphor. When lit with a fuse, they immediately let off a thick curtain of smoke enabling a dramatic escape. The amount of smoke and the manner in which the *enton* burned could be controlled by slight changes in the mixture.

Kannon-gakure God Hiding

To hide at night, disappear into the shadows or press yourself flat against a wall. Breathe as little as possible, cover your lower face with your sleeve, and to the rhythm of your racing heart silently chant the following -- "On Ah Ni Chi Ma Ri Shi E I So Wa Ka."

Uzura-gakure Quail Hiding

When hiding in a garden at night, wrap both arms over your head and crouch down like a quail-shape ball to resemble a garden stone.

Tanuki-gakure Badger Hiding

1 Choose the tallest and most leafy tree and scramble up.

2 To make the most of the branches and leaves, go deep into the tree.

3 Until your enemies leave, breathe as little as possible and don't move a muscle.

4 When they've gone, scramble down and make tracks.

Food, Shelter, Tricks, and Disguises

AT HOME AND AWAY

Staying on your tabi-toes anytime, anywhere.

NINJA IN THE HOUSE:LIFESTYLES OF THE DEADLY AND INVISIBLE

A spy's pad had to be customized.

At first glance, the ninja's house could be mistaken for any other -- that is, until it reveals its many secrets. There are places to hide from the enemy, holes to stash valuables in, trick doors, hidden passages, and concealed staircases. Some ninja houses even contained an extra secret floor.

Kakushi-kaidan
Hidden Staircase

Donden-gaeshi
Secret Door

Shikakedo
Trick Door

Karakuri-tobira
Mechanical Door

Mihariba
Lookout

Mono-kakushi
Hiding Place

Katana-kakushi
Hidden Sword

Donden-gaeshi Secret Door

At first, it looks like an ordinary wooden wall.

However, at the far left is a secret revolving door made of very light wood. Push on the wall here and you can disappear into a hidden space behind.

Once inside, you then swivel the door back, and nobody would know the difference.

Inside is a ladder made of thin strips of wood that leads to the second floor, while below the floorboards is a secret passage.

Kakushi-kaidan Hidden Staircase

The closet appears to contain nothing but a shelf.

But push the bottom center strut, and the shelf drops to reveal a hidden staircase.

From here you can climb to the second floor. In an escape, the floorboards can then be removed to leave a gaping hole.

Karakuri-tobira Mechanical Door

Pushing on the left side of the wall reveals the secret door. But push on the right side and nothing happens.

When danger threatened, the ninja could quickly scramble into the hidden space, sealing the door behind them.

Once inside, the wall can be pushed up, revealing a passage that leads under the family altar. The ninja could temporarily prop up the hatch with a sword to escape.

Shikakedo Trick Door

During a nighttime attack, having to open the heavy outer doors first would leave little time for escape.

Instead, they used a secret door to make their exit. Between the wall and the door, at the top and bottom, are two latches.

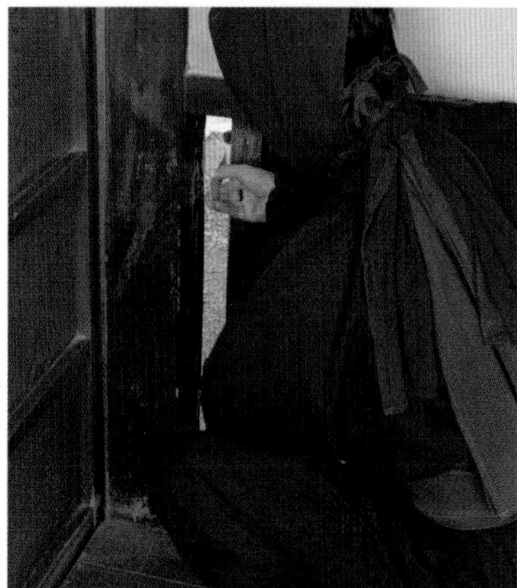

The escaping ninja would carry two sheets of card known as *kaeshi*. When inserted into special slots, the card would pop the latches, unlocking the door.

On the way out, they would push the hooks back to close the door and lock it tight.

Mihariba Lookout

Behind the sliding doors is a wall that contains a mechanical door.

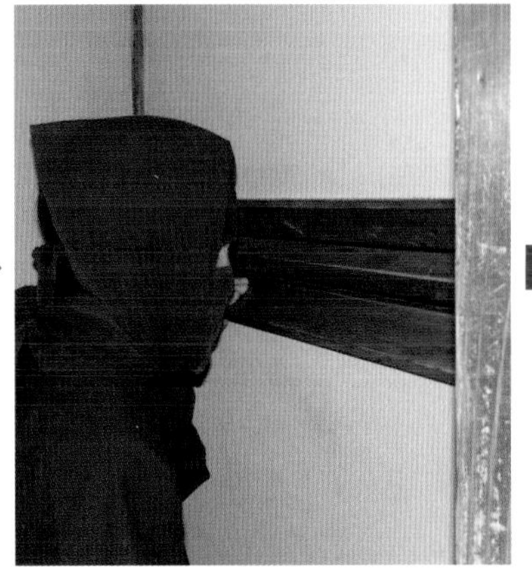

Behind this door is a space just large enough for one person.

Through this runs a three-sided wooden beam into which spyholes have been drilled. From these the ninja could survey the garden and surrounding fields undetected. From the dark of the room, the view of the outside is bright and clear.

Mono-kakushi Hiding Place

When you open the screen doors that are usually kept closed, you see the threshold. What you wouldn't notice is that the edge of one of these can be removed.

By removing the threshold, the floorboard can be lifted. Beneath is a layer of dry sand where the ninja would keep important documents and secret letters. In an escape, they could easily grab them and then hide them again once outside.

Katana-kakushi Hidden Sword

One floorboard closest to the roughest part of the threshold has been deliberately chosen to conceal a hiding place.

Below is a narrow space long enough to hold a sword.

Experiencing Ninja First Hand

Ninja Museum of the Iga Sect

Ninja Residence

There's a surprise, an ambush perhaps, then an escape through secret passages guided by a beautiful female ninja.

You can feel the ninja presence here, surrounded by the very tools and weapons they have touched and used.

The Hall of Ninja Folklore

Models of villages and houses where the ninja once lived offer a vivid picture of their homelife.

Behind the ninja mask was a person of learning. It's all here, their knowledge, their ancient texts, the tricks they used with such skill and cunning.

The museum is located in Ueno City, once the home of the Iga ninja sect, in Japan's Mie Prefecture. It serves as a reminder of the city's ninja roots.

Iga Ninja Sect Homepage
http://www.iganinja.jp/

The Hall of the Ninja

Visitors can even try on a pair of "mizugumo," which are the special shoes the ninja wore to cross swamps and marshlands.

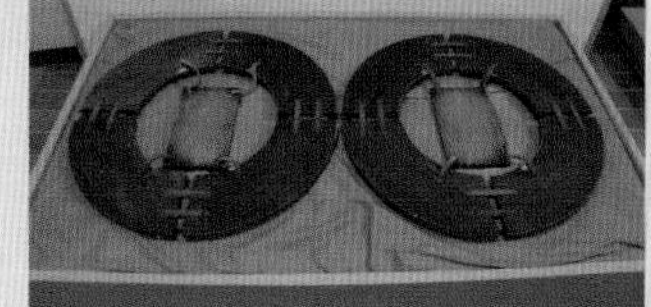

The ninja experience continues here, with over 400 displays dedicated to their craft, many which can be picked up and held.

Shuriken Throwing

Visitors also get to throw a few *shuriken*, the ninja weapon-of-choice. Although it's not as easy as it looks, you can really get into it.

Ninja Show

The Ninja Show brings it all to life. This impressively action-packed display of weaponry, including swordplay, is as real and as close as it gets.

THE NINJA DIET

You can't raid a castle on an empty stomach. An assassin throve on high-energy foods, and home-made *tofu* just like the Grand Master used to make.

Staple Food

The ninja diet consisted of high-protein foods, such as brown rice and wheat. This was supplemented with pickled plums, which help alleviate fatigue and cure infections. In the course of a day's work, the ninja would sometimes hang from a roof beam by only the thumbs and forefingers. To be able to do this, they had to keep their weight down. With a low calorie, high protein diet, men stayed around 132 pounds.

Other Ninja Foods

Sesame Seeds

To keep strong bones and healthy teeth, the ninja ate sesame seeds, which are high in vitamins and calcium.

Soybeans

The ninja were vegetarian, believing impurities in the blood would weaken their sixth sense. As a substitute for meat, they ate soybean *tofu*.

Quail Eggs

One ninja art is known as "quail hiding." They believed that eating quail eggs would enhance this method of camouflage.

Brown Sugar

The ninja snacked on sugar as an energy booster.

How to Make Ninja Tofu

As well as *tofu* being a low-calorie diet food, soybeans, its main ingredient, were once believed to have spiritual qualities.

Ingredients
(To make one large *tofu* block)

•Soybeans......300 g •Brine...... 20 cc

1 Wash the soybeans and place in 1.4 liters of water.

2 In a blender, mix the soybeans into the water until they become smooth and creamy. Stir and repeat two or three times.

3 Pour the soybean mix into a pot, add 200 cc of water, and heat over a strong flame. Bring to boil and then lower the heat. Let it simmer for another seven or eight minutes. To keep it from sticking, stir constantly.

4 Wrap the mix in a cotton cloth and wring it out over a pot. This juice is known as soya milk. Be careful. It's hot!

5 Heat the soya milk to about 70 degrees c°.

6 Dilute the brine in 40 cc of water and stir half of it into the soya milk. Place a cover over the pot and leave for 10 minutes. Then mix in the rest of the brine.

7 Line a large colander with a cotton cloth. Spoon in the hardened *tofu* mix.

8 Cover the mix with a folded cloth. Place a plate on top to weigh it down.

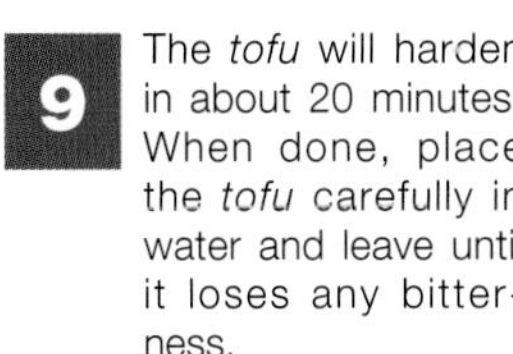

9 The *tofu* will harden in about 20 minutes. When done, place the *tofu* carefully in water and leave until it loses any bitterness.

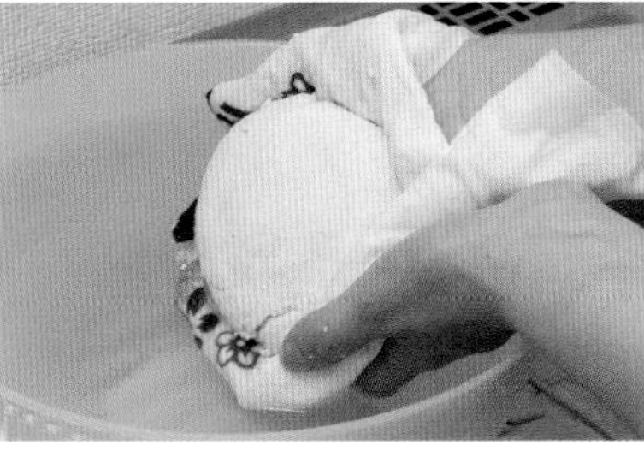

FINISH

Finally, cut the *tofu* and serve.

ASSASSIN WELLNESS

Rumbling with Ronin can take its toll. Accupressure and massage kept a ninja razor sharp.

Tsubo

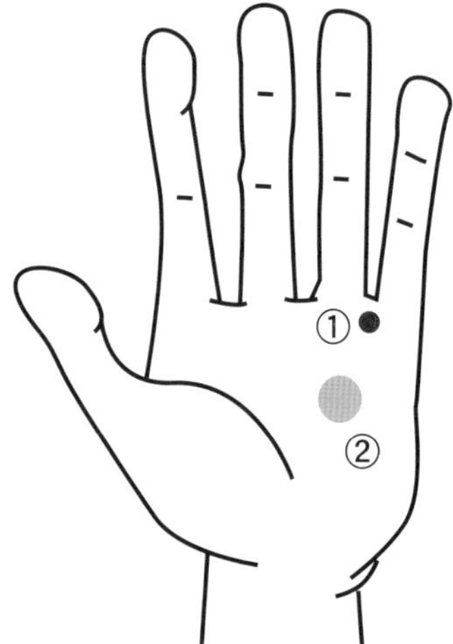

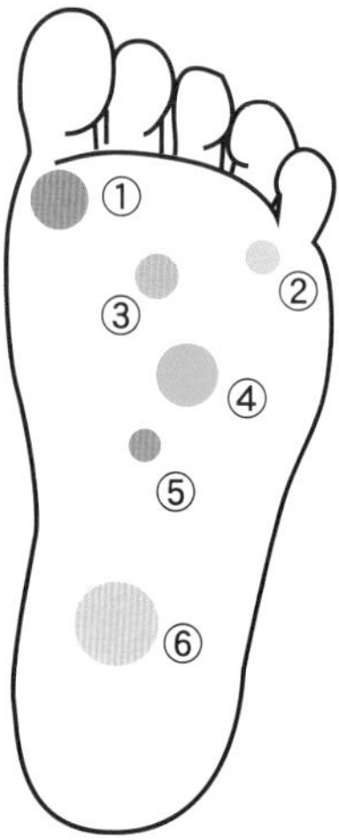

Pressure Points on the Hand

Pressure point (1) is known as the *ekimon* (small gate) point. It should be rubbed quite strongly with the outer side of the thumb. This point helps you to sweat out a fever. Pressure point (2) is known as the *jinzou*, or kidney point. Massaging this relieves swelling.

Pressure Points on the Feet

Stimulating pressure point (1) will relieve a stiff neck, (2) stiff shoulders, (3) tired lungs, (4) an overworked heart, (5) improves kidney function, and (6) is for the large intestine.

Toe Massage

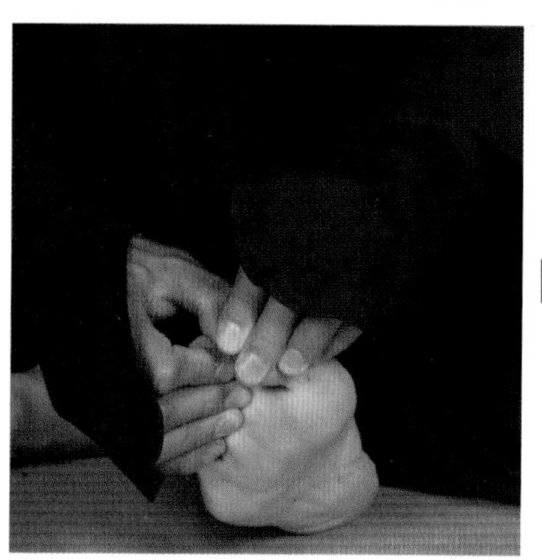

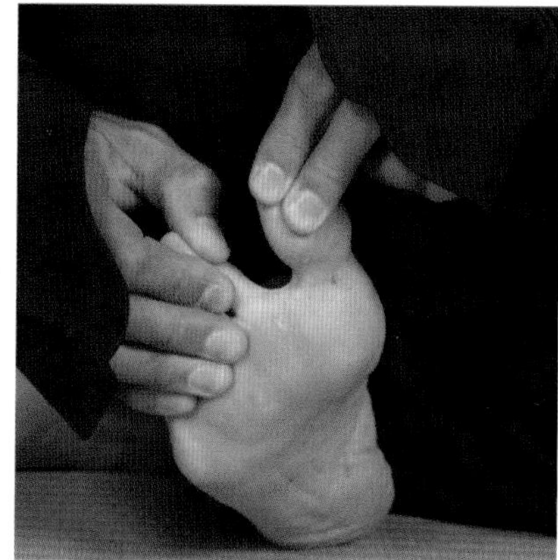

Massaging the big toe while bending it backwards and forwards was said to improve the performance of the liver. It also acts as a relaxant.

Hand Massage

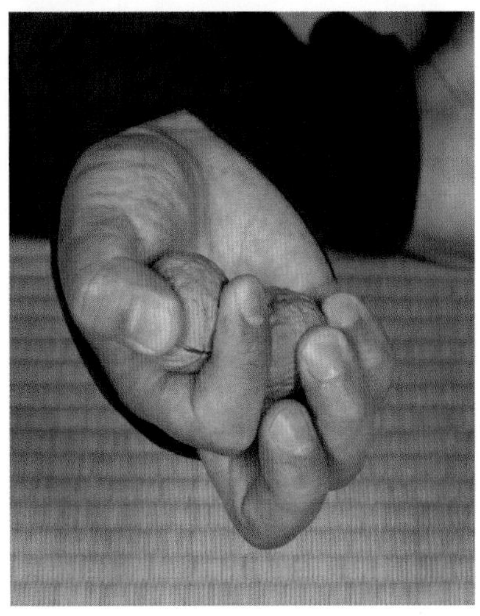

Hold two walnuts in the hand and turn them in a circular manner. The palm of the hand has numerous pressure points and stimulating them is meant to improve the body's organs.

Ear Massage

Rubbing the ear with the palm of the hand or pulling on it with the fingers improves the condition of the eyes, ears and internal organs.

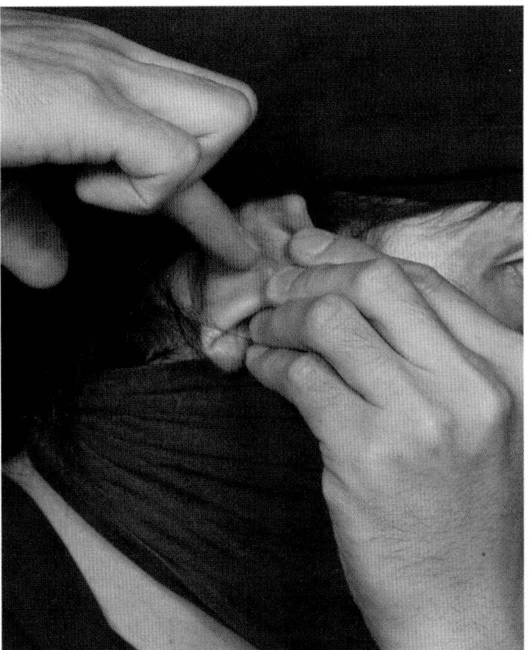

Flicking the back of the ear with the fingers improves hearing, makes the ears stronger, and soothes the head.

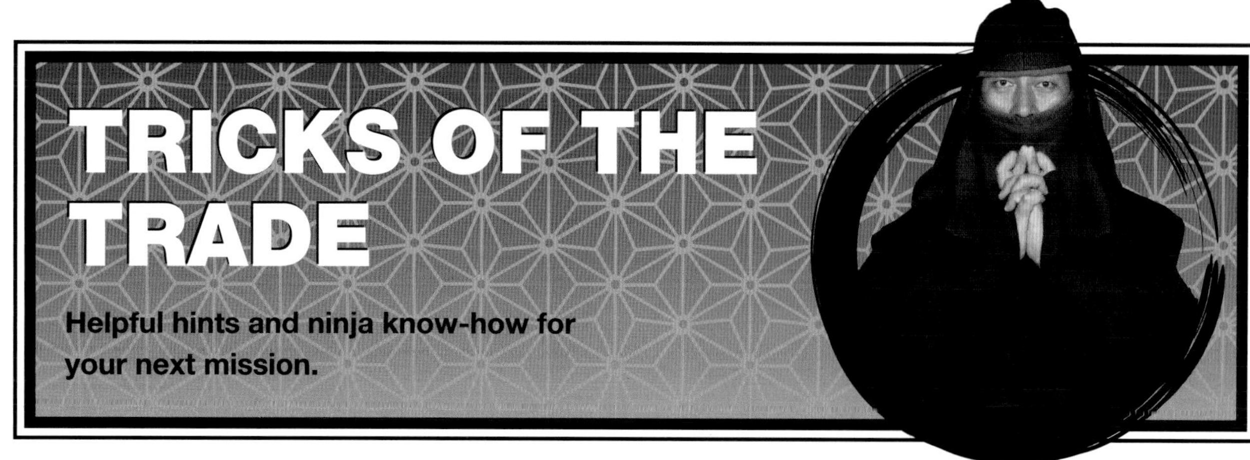

Telling the Time

In the days when clocks were still rare, people knew roughly what time of day or night it was by the position of the sun or the Big Dipper. The activities of certain animals, such as the dawn chorus, could also serve as something of a clock. The ever resourceful ninja, however, had their own system, known as the "Cat's Eye Clock."

Cat's Eye Clock

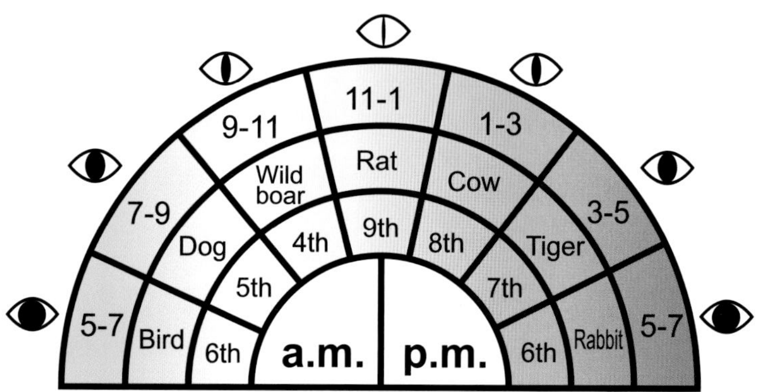

Staring into a cat's eyes, the ninja could calculate the time by studying the size of its pupils, which dilate and contract with the changing of the light. In the old days in Japan, the time was indicated by animal names, for example, "bird" is from 5AM to 7AM.

Weather Forecasting

Weather condition was an important factor for the ninja, who could turn the wind or rain to their advantage. Setting a castle on fire, for example, was best achieved when the wind was strong. When spying on somebody, however, the ninja prayed for rain, which would muffle any sound they made.

Forecasting the Weather

1. **Twinkling stars means rain is on its way.**
2. **If the mountains appear closer than usual, rain is sure to follow.**
3. **The moon's halo says rain is imminent.**
4. **Kites flying in downward circles suggest the following day will be wet.**
5. **When kites fly in ascending circles, the next day will be sunny.**
6. **Crows washing themselves in water means it's going to rain.**
7. **When water droplets appear on spider webs, the following day will be clear.**

Navigation

Although a compass can easily tell which direction is which, being caught with one was too much for the ninja to risk. They preferred to make their own with such inconspicuous items as a needle and wax. Also, on clear night, the polestar or the Big Dipper told the direction.

Making a Compass

Heat a needle until it glows red.

When it's red, immediately cool it in water.

Once cooled, pour wax over it.

The needle will now float. When placed in water, it will point North.

Finding Water

The ninja often found themselves stuck out in the wilds. Finding water, therefore, was vital for survival. For this they had a number of techniques, and if the water was dirty, they would simply filter it through a cloth. Yum.

How to Find Water

1. **Stick a crow's feather into the ground and wait. If it becomes damp then there's water below.**
2. **Dig in valleys where iris grow. There's sure to be water.**
3. **Place a towel on the floor of a cave. If it's wet the following day then there's a water source close by.**
4. **Dig a one-meter deep hole in the mountainside. Place your ear to the bottom and listen. If there's a sound it means there's water below.**
5. **Find an ant's nest. There'll be water nearby.**

Camping Out

1 To cook rice, the ninja first dug a hole.

2 The rice, which had been soaked in water for a few hours, was wrapped in a small towel.

3 They then buried the covered rice in the hole.

4 Over this they built a fire, which would cook the rice below. When done, they cleared away the fire, dug up the rice, and ate. To ward off animals, the fire was kept burning throughout the night.

5 On cold nights, they'd move the fire and sleep face-down on the heated ground in order to keep the heart, and therefore the body, as warm as possible.

When on the move, the ninja often had to camp out. Wild animals and cold nights meant bedding down outside was not without danger. The ninja's methods took advantage of what was on hand.

Delivering Secret Documents

Insho-hitoku-no-hou

1 The ninja would wrap thin strips of paper diagonally around a pole. They'd then write the secret messages onto the paper.

2 Once dry, they'd peel off the paper, leaving strips of illegible squiggle. This they would deliver to the recipient.

3 Once in the right hands, the reader would then wrap the paper strips around a pole of the same size, and read.

One of the ninja's many duties was to deliver secret documents. They used different methods to avoid discovery if inspected, such as memorizing the messages. In more extreme cases, they would shave their heads and carve the message into their scalps. Once their hair had grown back, they would deliver the message by shaving again once they arrived safely.

A FACE IN THE CROWD

The black suit does not always blend. Seven basic disguises let the ninja disappear in plain sight.

Hokashi

An entertainer, such as juggler, acrobat or monkey handler. You never can trust a man with a monkey.

Sarugakushi

A touring actor who sings, dances, and perfoms *kabuki* all over the country. Such people skipped through checkpoints with little trouble.

Yamabushi

A mountain ascetic, a hermit communing with nature on a mission of self-discovery. Cut off from society, these wild men weren't expected to carry permits.

The ninja's tasks included travelling the country gathering information. But regional checkpoints were introduced in the *Edo* era to prevent those without travel permits from moving freely from state to state. The ninja donned disguises to avoid detection while they continued their clandestine activities. These costumes known collectively as "*nanabake,*" would become their specialty.

Shonin

A travelling salesman shouldering an enormous bundle of medicines and candies from town to town. This itinerant profession enabled him to pass freely through checkpoints.

Shukke

A Buddhist monk. For this the ninja had to be able to chant the sutras as well. This disguise had an added bonus, however, as it allowed him a sneak peek at family registers, which at the time were administered by temples.

Komuso

A *shakuhachi*-playing priest in a long woven hood. The disguise was ideal, for as well as concealing his face, priests were allowed to pass through checkpoints without lifting their hoods.

Tsune-no-kata

A commoner, such as a farmer or a *samurai*. In this case the ninja had to be fluent in the local dialect and accent. He also needed a serious topknot.

WORDS OF WISDOM

THE WAY

1

Misuse of *Ninjutsu* is Forbidden

The ninja's loyalty is to the country and military commander they serve. They are forbidden to use *ninjutsu* for their own personal gain.

2

Overcoming Pride

The ninja's execution of their duties is paramount. Expending energy on personal disputes for pride is forbidden.

3

Leaking Secrets is Forbidden

The importance of the documents the ninja carries cannot be overstated. It is forbidden to discuss these with others.

4

Being Discovered is Forbidden

The ninja's work is secret. To perform their duties, they must remain hidden. It is forbidden to give oneself away.

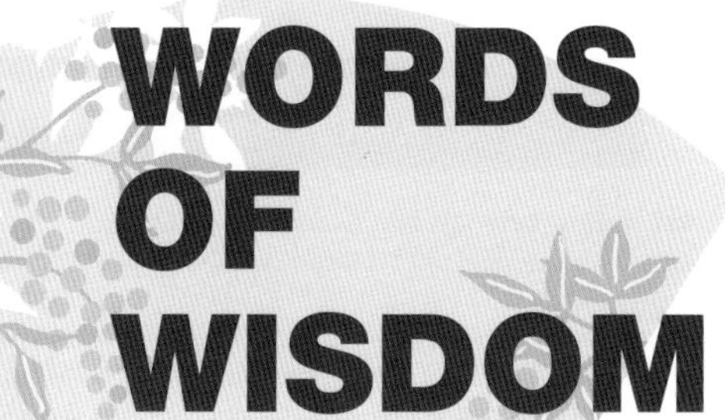

WORDS OF WISDOM

THE NAME OF THE NINJA

Ninja Names Through the Ages

Era		Name
Asuka-era	(574 ~ 709)	Shinobi
Nara-era	(710~ 793)	Ukami
Sengoku-era	(1192 ~ 1602)	Kanjya, Kyoudan, Rappa, Mitsumono, Kenen
Edo-era	(1603 ~ 1868)	Onmitsu, Oniwaban

The name "ninja" is in fact a recent title. In past eras the ninja had different names, and sometimes no name at all.

Ninja Names According to Region

Region	Name
Kyoto / Nara	Suppa, Ukami, Dakkou, Shinobi
Aomori	Hayamichinomono, Shinobi
Miyagi	Kurohabaki
Kanagawa	Kusa, Kamari, Monomi, Rappa, Toppa
Tokyo	Onmitsu, Oniwaban
Yamanashi	Mitsumono, Suppa, Sukinami, Denuki
Aichi	Kyoudan
Fukui	Shinobi
Niigata / Toyama	Nokizaru, Kyoudou, Kyoudan, Kanshi, Kikimonoyaku

Because words and dialects vary from region to region, ninja were known by a number of names.

WORDS OF WISDOM PHRASEBOOK

B

bansenshukai [ban-sen-shu-kai] *noun.* A 22-volume ninja manual written by *Iga* native Fujibayashi Yasutake. It contained 49 tenets of *Iga* and *Koka ninjutsu.*
Basho Matsuo [basho matsuo] *name.* 1644~1694.Famous *haiku* poet, whose works included The Narrow Roads to Far Towns. He spent many years walking around Japan penning *haiku.* He was born in *Iga*, and on his travels covered 40 to 50 km in a day. Where he got his money to travel from remains a mystery, and legend has it that he was in fact a ninja.
bureimono [bu-ray-mo-no] *noun.* To be against etiquette. Something or someone discourteous.

C

chito [chi-to] *adv.* Referred to a little or a few.
chonmage [chon-ma-geh] *noun. Edo* period hairstyle for men. The head was shaved above the forehead and the hair at the back tied in a top-knot.

Danzo Kato [danzo kato] *name.* Ninja. Date of birth and death unknown. Known also as "Tobi Kato" or "Flying Kato." He was said to have practiced sorcery and had the ability to control people through hypnosis. His alias comes from his alledged ability to fly. The Warring States era military commander, Uesugi Kenshin, attempted to use his secret powers and tested his *ninjutsu*, but Kato was so good he was a threat to Uesugi. Uesugi tried to kill him, but sensing the danger, Kato went over to Uesugi's rival, Takeda Shingen. The same things happened, but this time Kato was killed. There are many versions of this story, and many mysteries surrounding Kato.
doron [doh-ron] *noun.* To suddenly disappear without notice. The origin of the Ninja's *enton* (smoke stick).

Ennogyojya [ennogyoja] *name.* Date of birth and death unknown. Sorcerer. Also known as Ennoozune. Active in the late 7th century, he was an originator of *shugendo*, a practice followed by mountain ascetics who lived deep in the mountains under a regimen that pushed their minds and bodies to the extreme. Through this they would hope to receive omens. One disguise that the ninja favored was that of a mountain ascetic.

gozaru [go-zaru] *verb.* Polite form of "There is..." or "There are..." More familiar than *"soro."*
gyoi [gyo-i] *noun.* Used when agreeing with the opinions of those of higher social status.

Hanzo Hattori [hanzo hattori] *name.* 1542~1596. One of the most famous ninja. Because of his help in rescuing the captured family of Warring States era general, Tokugawa Ieyasu, he was chosen as his ninja chief. Below him he had a force of 200 men involved in intelligence work. However Hattori's real figure was one of combat commander of his own battalion.
hori [hori] *noun.* Moat around a castle, filled either with water or mud to deter an attack. The bridge across it that led to the castle would be raised at night.

ikusa [i-ku-sa] *noun.* War, battle

kashira [ka-shi-ra] *noun.* Leader of one faction within a group. Relatively impolite.
katajike nai [kata-ji-keh-nai] *adj.* Extremely grateful.
kawaya [ka-wa-ya] *noun.* Toliet. Outhouse placed at a short distance from the family quarters.
Kotaro Fuma [kotaro fuma] *name.* Ninja. Date of birth and death unknown. Leader of the *Fuma* Ninja group employed by Hojo Ujinao. A huge man with a fierce face and exceptional *ninjutsu* skills, in stories he is often portrayed as a monster.
kuse mono [ku-seh-mono] *noun.* Someone suspicious, who cannot be trusted, or indicating someone hard to figure out.
Kuuemon [ku-u-e-mon] *name.* Ninja. Date of birth and death unknown. When sent to assasinate a certain lord, he sneaked into the ceiling but he was found and stabbed in his forehead with a spear through the ceiling. However, he didn't make any noise, wiped the blood from his face, and awaited another chance. He was then successful in the assassination. Because of the scar on his head, he became known as "Ana (hole) Kuuemon."

mawasi mono [mawa-shi-mono] *noun.* A mole who attempts to discover what orders have been passed down from his boss. A spy.
mete [meh-teh] *noun.* The left hand. Literally, "the hand that holds the reins."

oniwaban [oni-wa-ban] *noun.* The system established by 8th Shogun, Tokugawa Yoshimune, that placed ninja under the direct control of the *Edo Bakufu* government.
onushi [onu-shi] *pron.*"You" when speaking to those of the same social level, or lower.

samurai [samu-rai] *noun.*The general term used for those warriors involved in military affairs who had studied the martial arts. Although a completely different kind people from the ninja, they too served *daimyo* and the *shogun.*
sayou [sa-yo-u] *adv.*"That's right," or "That's it."
seikan [say-kan] *noun.* A ninja who returns alive from enemy territory with important information. Literally, "between life."
sessya [say-shha] *pron.*"I" when speaking with humility to those of the same social level, or lower.
shikan [shi-kan] *noun.* Someone prepared to risk their life in order to infiltrate enemy territory and spread false information. Literally, "between death."
soti, sonata [so-chi, so-nata] *pron.* "You!" to someone who is of a lower status.
sourou [so-u-ro-u] *verb.* Polite way to say "There is..." or "There are..."

tentyu [ten-tyu] *noun.* Punishment from Heaven. Also, to take the place of Heaven to dispense punishment.
tono [toh-no] *noun.* Ruler's title of honor.
torimono dougu [tori-mono-doh-gu] *noun.* Weapon used by the *Edo* era police force. Commonly known as *yoriki* or *doshin*, it would injure but not kill the suspect, enabling him to be taken into custody.
tou [toh] *noun.* General term used to refer to family or intimates living or working together. The ninja's practice was organized by each *tou*, which was passed down from parents to children.

yatou [ya-toh] *noun.* Robbery, or the act of sneaking into the enemy camp at night and stealing something.
yunde [yun-deh] *noun.* The right hand. Literally, "The hand that holds the bow."

INDEX